Emotional Roller Coaster

Emotional Roller Coaster

Emotional Roller Coaster

Helping teens navigate emotional highs and lows

By Whitney Williams

Emotional Roller Coaster

Emotional Roller Coaster

Helping teens navigate emotional highs and lows
Copyright © 2024 by Whitney Williams
All rights reserved.

No part of this publication may be reproduced, distributed, or transmitted in any form or by any means, including photocopying, recording, or other electronic or mechanical methods, without the prior written permission of the publisher, except in the case of brief quotations embodied in critical reviews and certain other noncommercial uses permitted by copyright law.

For permission requests, write to the publisher at:
Whitneywilliamswrites@gmail.com

This book is a work of the author's experience and research. It is intended for informational and educational purposes only. The content should not be used as a substitute for professional medical or mental health advice. If you or someone you know is struggling with emotional or mental health concerns, please consult a healthcare professional.
First Edition: August 2024

Emotional Roller Coaster

To every teen who has ever felt confused, overwhelmed, or unsure about their emotions you are not alone. This book is for you.
And to my family and friends, thank you for always supporting me through all of my own feelings.

Emotional Roller Coaster

Introduction

Welcome to Emotional Roller Coaster! If you've ever felt overwhelmed by your emotions or confused about what you're feeling, this book is for you. Growing up can be tough, especially when you're dealing with new and sometimes intense emotions. But here's the good news: it's totally normal to experience a wide range of feelings, and you're not alone. This book will help you understand your emotions and give you practical ways to handle them.

Each chapter explores different emotions—like happiness, sadness, anger, and anxiety—and includes activities that will help you get in touch with how you're feeling. You'll find journal prompts, affirmations, and real life scenarios where you can reflect on what you would do. These interactive exercises are designed to help you make sense of your emotions and build healthier habits for managing them.

Feel free to take your time with each section. There's no right or wrong way to use this book. Whether you're feeling great or going through a tough time, this guide is here to help you better understand yourself and the emotions you're experiencing. You can skip around, focus on the sections that resonate most with you, or even share your thoughts with a trusted friend or adult.

Most importantly, remember that your feelings matter. Emotions can be messy, but they also make us who we are. So, as you work through the pages of this book, know that you are building a stronger connection with yourself, and that's something to be proud of.

Let's ride this emotional roller coaster, together!

Chapter 1: You're Not Alone

Hey there. Let's be real for a second—being a teenager is a wild ride. One minute, you're on top of the world, and the next, it feels like everything's falling apart. Whether you're dealing with school stress, friend drama, or just trying to figure out who you are, it's a lot. And guess what? That's totally okay.

Let me tell you something that might surprise you: everyone has feelings. And I don't mean just the "happy" or "excited" ones. I'm talking about the confusing, upsetting, and overwhelming ones too. Maybe you've felt like you're the only one who gets anxious before a big test or cries after a rough day. But the truth is, those feelings are as normal as it gets.

Think about it this way—emotions are like a really intense weather system. Some days, everything's sunny and warm. Other days, it's a full-on thunderstorm with lightning, wind, and maybe even some hail. Just like the weather, your emotions change, and sometimes you're not even sure why. And that's perfectly fine.

But here's the thing: just because it's normal doesn't mean it's easy. It can be super frustrating to feel like you're on an emotional rollercoaster with no way to get off. Maybe you've tried to push your feelings down, or ignore them, hoping they'll just go away. Spoiler alert: they don't. The more you try to avoid your feelings, the louder they get. They're like that one song that gets stuck in your head—no matter how much you try to ignore it, it just keeps playing on repeat.

So, what do you do? First, take a deep breath. Seriously, do it. Right now. Breathe in, and let it out slowly. Feel a little better? Good. Now, let's talk about why it's so important to understand and accept your emotions, even the tough ones.

Emotions are your body's way of telling you something important. When you're sad, it's a signal that something isn't right. When you're angry, it's your brain's way of saying, "Hey, something needs to change!" And when you're happy, well, that's your body's way of celebrating. Each emotion has a purpose, even the ones that feel messy or uncomfortable.

But here's the best part: you're not alone in this. Every single person you know—your friends, your family, even that super confident girl at school—goes through this. They have their own thunderstorms and sunny days, just like you. The key is learning how to navigate those feelings so they don't take over your life. And that's exactly what this book is here to help you with.

We're going to explore all kinds of emotions—anxiety, sadness, anger, love—and figure out how to deal with them in a healthy way. There's no one-size-fits-all answer, but by the end of this book, you'll have some tools in your emotional toolkit to help you handle whatever comes your way.

So, buckle up! This journey through your emotions might get a little bumpy, but trust me, it's worth it. After all, feelings are what make us human.

Emotional Roller Coaster

You're Not Alone

Maya sat in the cafeteria, nervously poking at her lunch. The big school showcase was just two days away, and her anxiety was starting to feel overwhelming. Her friends, Aisha, Brooke, and Jenna, all seemed calm, laughing and chatting about their weekend plans, but Maya couldn't shake the feeling that she was the only one who was freaking out.

The thought of performing her poem in front of the whole school made her palms sweaty. *What if I forget the words?* she thought. *What if my voice shakes?* She glanced at her friends and wondered, *Why does it feel like I'm the only one struggling?*

"Maya, you okay?" Aisha's voice snapped her out of her thoughts.

"Yeah, just… tired, I guess," Maya muttered, forcing a smile. She didn't want to admit how anxious she really felt. They'd probably think she was overreacting.

Later that night, as Maya lay in bed, she stared at her phone. Should she text them? Should she let them know how she felt? After a few moments, she typed out a message in their group chat: *Hey, does anyone else feel nervous about the showcase? I can't stop freaking out about it.*

She stared at the screen, heart pounding, and almost deleted the message, but before she could, a reply from Brooke popped up: *Omg, yes! I've been practicing all week, but I still feel like I'm going to mess up my lines.*

Then Aisha chimed in: *Same here. I can't even sleep, thinking about the dance routine. I'm terrified I'll mess up in front of everyone.*

Maya blinked at the screen in surprise. *Wait, you guys feel anxious too?* she typed.

Definitely, Jenna replied. *I've been so worried about my artwork being judged. What if no one likes it?*

Maya felt a wave of relief wash over her. She had been so convinced that she was the only one struggling, but now she realized her friends were feeling just like she was.

Wow, Maya typed, *I thought I was the only one. It's kind of nice knowing I'm not alone.*

Brooke responded: *We've all got our stuff. We just don't always talk about it.*

Maya smiled at her phone. Maybe she didn't have to handle this all by herself. The next day, when she saw her friends at school, there was an unspoken understanding between them. It didn't erase Maya's anxiety, but knowing she wasn't alone made it easier to manage.

The day of the showcase, when Maya stood on stage, her hands were still shaking, but she took a deep breath and glanced at her friends in the front row. They were all dealing with their own nerves, and somehow, that made her feel a little braver.

When the words of her poem flowed out, her voice didn't shake as much as she thought it would.

Message: Everyone has their own emotional struggles, even if they don't show it. It's okay to reach out for help and share how you're feeling.

Emotional Roller Coaster

Chapter 2: Dealing with Anxiety – "When Your Brain Won't Turn Off"

Let's talk about something that's probably visited you at some point—anxiety. You know, that nagging feeling in your chest that makes it hard to breathe, or that voice in your head that won't stop replaying worst-case scenarios. Yeah, that. It's like your brain decides to throw a wild party, but instead of fun and games, it's filled with worries and what-ifs.

What Is Anxiety, Anyway?

Anxiety is a totally normal emotion that everyone experiences at some point. It's your brain's way of responding to stress or danger. Think of it as your body's built-in alarm system. When you're about to give a big presentation or you hear a strange noise in the middle of the night, your brain sends out a signal: *"Hey, something's up. Get ready to deal with this!"* That signal is anxiety, and in small doses, it's actually helpful. It keeps you alert and focused.

But here's the catch—sometimes, that alarm system goes off even when there's no real danger. Maybe it happens when you're sitting in class, trying to concentrate on a math problem, but all you can think about is whether you'll pass the test. Or maybe you're lying in bed at night, and suddenly you're wide awake, worrying about something that happened days ago. That's when anxiety stops being helpful and starts being a pain.

Common Triggers of Anxiety

Anxiety can be triggered by all sorts of things. Here are a few common ones you might recognize:

- School Stress:
  Tests, homework, and the pressure to do well can make your anxiety levels spike.

- Social Situations:
  Walking into a room full of people, public speaking, or just worrying about what others think of you can be major anxiety triggers.

- Change:
  Whether it's moving to a new school, changes in your family, or even just starting a new routine, change can make you feel anxious.

- Perfectionism:
  If you're always aiming for perfection and afraid of making mistakes, anxiety can hit hard when things don't go as planned.

- Uncertainty:
  Not knowing what's going to happen next, like waiting for test results or dealing with the unknown, can set off anxiety.

- These triggers can make you feel like your brain is stuck on overdrive, constantly worrying about things that might go wrong. It's exhausting, right?

Practical Strategies to Manage Anxiety

The good news is, you don't have to let anxiety run the show. Here are some practical strategies to help you manage it:

- Breathe Deeply:
   When anxiety hits, your breathing often becomes shallow and fast, which only makes things worse. Try this: take a slow, deep breath in through your nose, hold it for a few seconds, and then slowly breathe out through your mouth.

Repeat this a few times. It might sound simple, but deep breathing sends a signal to your brain that it's okay to relax.

- Ground Yourself:
  When your thoughts start spiraling, grounding exercises can help bring you back to the present moment. Try the "5-4-3-2-1" method:
  - Name 5 things you can see.
  - Name 4 things you can touch.
  - Name 3 things you can hear.
  - Name 2 things you can smell.
  - Name 1 thing you can taste.

This technique can help distract your mind from anxious thoughts and focus on the here and now.

- Write It Down:
  Sometimes, putting your worries on paper can make them feel less overwhelming. Keep a journal where you can unload your thoughts, or even make a list of what's bothering you. Seeing your worries written out can help you realize that they're manageable.

- Talk to Someone:
  You don't have to deal with anxiety alone. Talking to a friend, family member, or someone you trust can be incredibly helpful. Sometimes just saying your worries out loud can make them feel less scary. And who knows? They might even have some good advice or just the right words to make you feel better.

- Move Your Body:
  Physical activity is a great way to burn off nervous energy. Whether it's going for a run, dancing around your room, or even just taking a walk, moving your body can help clear your mind and reduce anxiety.

- Limit Caffeine and Sugar:
  Caffeine and sugar can make anxiety worse by speeding up your heart rate and making you feel jittery. Try to keep your intake in check, especially if you're already feeling anxious.

- Create a "Worry Time":
  If you find yourself worrying all the time, set aside a specific time each day to focus on your worries. Spend 10-15 minutes thinking about what's bothering you, and then once that time

is up, move on to something else. This can help keep anxiety from taking over your entire day.

- Practice Self-Compassion:
Be kind to yourself. It's easy to get frustrated or feel like you're "failing" when anxiety hits, but remember that it's a part of being human. Treat yourself with the same kindness and understanding you would offer a friend who's struggling.

Remember, You've Got This

Anxiety can feel like a giant weight on your chest, but remember—you're stronger than you think. By understanding what anxiety is and using these strategies, you can start to take control and make it through those tough moments. And the best part? The more you practice, the easier it gets.

So, the next time your brain won't turn off, try one of these strategies. It might not make the anxiety disappear completely, but it can help you feel more in control, and that's a pretty big win.

Finding Calm

Emma sat at her desk, staring at the pile of textbooks in front of her. The math test was tomorrow, she still had an essay to finish, and there was a science project due next week. It felt like everything was crashing down at once. Her mind was spinning with all the things she had to do, and she didn't know where to start.

What if I fail the test? What if I forget everything I studied? Emma's chest tightened, and she felt like she couldn't breathe. She glanced at her phone, feeling like she needed to talk to someone, but didn't know who to call. Her parents wouldn't understand—they always expected her to do well in school—and her friends were probably too busy with their own homework.

Suddenly, her phone buzzed. It was a text from her older cousin, Sarah: *Hey, just checking in! How's everything going?*

Emma hesitated for a moment before replying: *Honestly? I'm kind of freaking out right now. I've got so much to do, and I don't know how to handle it.*

Almost immediately, Sarah responded: *Wanna talk?*

Emma quickly dialed her cousin, feeling a sense of relief that Sarah had reached out. When Sarah picked up, her calm voice instantly made Emma feel a little better.

"I feel like I'm drowning," Emma confessed. "I've got this huge test, projects, and assignments. It's just too much."

"I've been there," Sarah said. "I know how overwhelming school can get. It feels like if you don't stay on top of everything, it'll all come crashing down."

"Exactly," Emma said, her voice shaky. "But how do you deal with it? I just feel stuck."

"I used to get really anxious about school too," Sarah explained. "It got so bad that I couldn't focus. But I learned some techniques that helped me manage the stress. Want to try a grounding exercise?"

"Uh, sure," Emma said, not really knowing what that meant.

"Okay, let's start with deep breathing," Sarah said gently. "Close your eyes and take a deep breath in for four counts, hold it for four, and then slowly breathe out for four. Do that a few times."

Emma did as she was told. After a few deep breaths, the tightness in her chest began to loosen.

"Now," Sarah continued, "look around the room. Can you name five things you can see?"

Emma glanced around her room. "My backpack, the lamp, my bookshelf, my poster, and...my pencil case."

"Good. Now, can you name four things you can touch?"

Emma ran her fingers along her desk. "My desk, my sweater, my chair, and my notebook."

"Now three things you can hear?"

"The clock ticking, the sound of cars outside, and...my breathing."

"Great job. How do you feel now?"

Emotional Roller Coaster

Emma opened her eyes and realized her mind wasn't racing anymore. "I feel...calmer. I didn't know that could work."

"It helps when things get overwhelming," Sarah said. "Another thing that helped me was journaling. I would write down everything I was worried about, just to get it out of my head. It made things seem less scary."

"That sounds like something I could try," Emma said. "I've never thought of writing about how I feel."

"Trust me, it helps," Sarah assured her. "And remember, it's okay to talk about your worries. Everyone feels anxious sometimes, even if they don't show it."

Emma nodded, feeling a wave of relief. "Thanks, Sarah. I really needed this."

"Anytime," Sarah replied. "And don't hesitate to reach out whenever you're feeling like this. You're not alone."

As Emma hung up the phone, she sat down with her notebook and began writing. With each word, the weight she'd been carrying began to lift. She wasn't spiraling anymore. She had tools to help her, and she knew it was okay to ask for help.

Message: Anxiety is something everyone experiences at times. Techniques like deep breathing, grounding exercises, and journaling can help you feel more in control. It's important to talk about your feelings and not carry the burden alone.

Emotional Roller Coaster

What would you do?

These scenarios are designed to help you think about practical strategies for managing anxiety in different situations and to encourage you to apply the coping mechanisms discussed in the chapter.

Scenario 1: The Overwhelming Exam

You have a major exam coming up, and you can't stop worrying about whether you'll do well. Despite studying, you find it hard to focus because your mind keeps racing with anxious thoughts about the exam.
What would you do to calm your anxiety and improve your focus?

_____
_____
_____
_____

Scenario 2: The Social Event

You're invited to a large social event, but the thought of being in a big crowd makes you feel extremely anxious. You're worried about what people will think of you and whether you'll be able to socialize comfortably.

What strategies would you use to manage your anxiety and make the event more manageable?

_____
_____
_____
_____

Scenario 3: The Endless To-Do List

Your to-do list seems never-ending, and you feel overwhelmed by all the tasks you need to complete. The pressure of staying on top of everything is causing you significant stress and anxiety.

How would you prioritize your tasks and manage your anxiety to handle your to-do list effectively?

_____
_____
_____
_____

Scenario 4: The Upcoming Presentation

You have to give a presentation in front of your class, and you're feeling anxious about speaking publicly. Your mind keeps replaying worst-case scenarios, making it hard for you to prepare and feel confident.
What techniques would you use to reduce your anxiety and prepare for the presentation?

_____
_____
_____
_____

Scenario 5: The Personal Conflict

You've had a disagreement with a close friend, and you can't stop replaying the argument in your mind. You're anxious about how it might affect your relationship and how to resolve the conflict.
What steps would you take to manage your anxiety and address the conflict with your friend?

_____
_____
_____
_____

Emotional Roller Coaster

Chapter 3: Handling Sadness
"It's Okay to Cry"

Sadness. It's one of those feelings that no one really likes to talk about, but everyone experiences. You know the feeling—your chest feels heavy, your eyes sting with tears, and all you want to do is curl up in bed and shut out the world. Whether it's because of a fight with a friend, a bad grade, or something deeper, sadness is a part of life. And guess what? That's okay.

What Is Sadness, and Why Do We Feel It?

Sadness is a natural response to loss, disappointment, or anything that doesn't go the way you hoped. It's your body's way of processing emotions when things don't feel right. While happiness feels like sunshine and laughter, sadness feels like clouds and rain. And just like we need rain for plants to grow, sometimes we need sadness to grow emotionally.

Sadness can happen for many reasons. Maybe you didn't get picked for the team, or you're feeling lonely, or something bigger is going on at home. Whatever the cause, sadness is a signal that something is important to you. It's your heart's way of saying, "This matters, and I'm hurting." But sadness isn't just about tears and gloomy days. It can show up in different ways, like feeling tired, losing interest in things you usually love, or even getting irritated easily. Sometimes, you might not even know why you're sad—it's just there, like a shadow that won't go away. And that's okay too.

Coping with Sadness: How to Ride Out the Storm

Just like any storm, sadness doesn't last forever. But while it's here, it's important to find ways to cope. Here are some strategies that can help:

- Let It Out:
  Crying isn't a sign of weakness—it's actually a natural way for your body to release stress and emotions. If you feel like crying, don't hold back. Find a quiet place where you feel comfortable, and let those tears flow. You'll probably feel a little lighter afterward.

- Talk to Someone:
  When you're sad, it can feel like you're all alone in the world. But you're not. Reach out to someone you trust—a friend, family member, or even a teacher—and tell them how you're feeling. You don't have to go into all the details if you're not ready, but just sharing that you're feeling down can make a big difference.

- Write It Down:
  Sometimes, putting your feelings into words can help you make sense of them. Grab a journal or a piece of paper and start writing about what's making you sad. You don't have to worry about grammar or spelling—just let your thoughts flow. Writing can be a great way to release emotions and see things more clearly.

- Do Something You Enjoy:
  When you're sad, it's easy to lose interest in things you usually love. But sometimes, doing something you enjoy can help lift your spirits, even if it's just a little. Whether it's listening to your favorite music, drawing, or watching a movie you love, give yourself permission to enjoy those things, even if you don't feel 100% into it at first.

- Get Moving:
  Physical activity might be the last thing you want to do when you're sad, but it can actually help. Going for a walk, dancing around your room, or even just stretching can boost your mood and help you feel a little better. Movement releases endorphins—your body's natural "feel good" chemicals—which can help take the edge off your sadness.

- Practice Self-Compassion:
  When you're sad, it's easy to start being hard on yourself. You might think, "Why can't I just get over this?" But beating yourself up won't make you feel better. Instead, try being kind to yourself. Imagine what you would say to a friend who's feeling sad, and then say those things to yourself. It's okay to be gentle with yourself when you're hurting.

- Remember That It's Okay to Feel Sad:
  Sadness is a normal part of life. It's okay to feel sad, and it's okay to take time to heal. You don't have to force yourself to be happy or "get over it" quickly. Healing takes time, and everyone's timeline is different. Give yourself the space to feel what you're feeling without judgment.

Heres to Finding Light in the Darkness

Sadness might feel overwhelming at times, but it's important to remember that it won't last forever. Just like the sun eventually breaks through the clouds, your sadness will lift. And when it does, you'll emerge stronger and more resilient.

Remember, it's okay to cry. It's okay to feel sad. And it's okay to ask for help when you need it. By acknowledging your sadness and finding ways to cope, you're taking important steps toward healing and growth.

And don't forget—you're not alone. Everyone feels sad sometimes, and it's nothing to be ashamed of. So, the next time those clouds roll in, know that you have the strength to weather the storm and come out on the other side.

Emotional Roller Coaster

Tears and Growth

Zoe sat on the edge of her bed, staring at her phone. The text messages between her and her best friend, Taylor, felt like a punch in the gut. They had argued over something small that spiraled into a full-blown fight, and now, they weren't speaking. Zoe had spent the last hour replaying their conversation in her head, wondering where things had gone so wrong.

Her chest felt heavy, and she fought back the urge to cry. She wasn't the type to let her emotions out like that, even when everything felt like it was crumbling. Instead, she pulled her knees to her chest and stared blankly at the wall.

A soft knock came at her door, and her grandmother, who was visiting for the weekend, peeked her head in. "Mind if I come in?"

Zoe shrugged, not trusting her voice to answer. Her grandmother sat beside her, not saying anything for a while. She just placed a gentle hand on Zoe's shoulder.

"I saw the look on your face earlier," her grandmother said quietly. "What's going on, sweetie?"

Zoe's throat tightened, but she didn't want to talk about it. She didn't want to seem weak. "It's nothing, Grandma."

Her grandmother smiled gently. "You don't have to say anything if you're not ready. But I've learned that holding in your sadness only makes it heavier."

Zoe's eyes started to burn with unshed tears. "It's just... I had a fight with Taylor. She was my best friend, and now we're not even speaking. I don't know what to do." Her voice cracked, and she quickly wiped at her eyes, trying to keep herself together.

Her grandmother's expression softened. "I'm sorry to hear that. Losing a friend, even temporarily, can feel like losing a part of yourself."

Zoe nodded, biting her lip to keep from crying, but her grandmother continued, "You know, when I was your age, I had a falling out with my best friend too. Her name was Clara, and we had a big argument over a boy. We stopped talking, and for months, I felt lost."

Zoe looked up, surprised. "What did you do?"

Her grandmother chuckled softly. "I cried—a lot. I used to think crying was weak, but I learned that it's actually a way to heal. I let myself feel the sadness, and after a while, it didn't hurt so much anymore. Over time, I found comfort in small things—like taking walks, baking, and reading. And eventually, Clara and I talked again. We weren't the same, but I grew stronger because of that experience."

Zoe felt a tear slip down her cheek, and this time, she didn't try to stop it. Her grandmother pulled her into a hug.

"It's okay to cry, Zoe," her grandmother whispered. "Crying doesn't mean you're weak—it means you're human. Sometimes, we need to grieve the things we've lost, even if it's just a friendship for now."

Zoe's tears started to fall faster, and she let them. She cried for the argument, for the friendship that felt broken, and for the sadness she had been holding in. Her grandmother held her until the sobs slowed.

"Do you feel a little lighter now?" her grandmother asked when Zoe finally pulled back.

Zoe nodded. "Yeah, I do. I didn't realize how much I needed to just let it out."

Her grandmother smiled. "Sometimes, we don't. But remember, you don't have to go through these feelings alone. It's always good to talk to someone you trust. And don't forget to take comfort in small things—whatever brings you peace, even if it's just for a little while."

Zoe wiped her face, feeling calmer. "Thanks, Grandma. I guess I was scared of being sad."

"It's okay to feel sad," her grandmother said gently. "Sadness isn't the end—it's a part of growing. You'll come out of this stronger."

As her grandmother left the room, Zoe glanced out the window and noticed the way the evening light streamed through the trees, casting a warm glow. She took a deep breath, feeling the weight on her chest lift just a little. Maybe, just maybe, it was okay to let herself feel sad sometimes.

And maybe, with time, she would grow from it.

Emotional Roller Coaster

Message: Crying is a healthy and natural way to release emotions. It's okay to grieve when you're feeling lost, and finding comfort in small things or talking to someone you trust can help you through it. Sadness can lead to personal growth if we let ourselves feel it.

Emotional Roller Coaster

Chapter 4: Taming the Inner Critic – "Building Your Confidence, One Step at a Time"

Let's dive into something that just about everyone struggles with at some point: self-esteem. Whether it's worrying about how you look, feeling like you're not good enough, or comparing yourself to others, low self-esteem can be a huge roadblock. But here's the good news—you're not stuck with it. Self-esteem is like a muscle, and with a little effort, you can make it stronger.

What Is Self-Esteem?

Self-esteem is basically how you see yourself and how much you value your own worth. It's that voice in your head that tells you whether you're awesome or not so much. When your self-esteem is high, you feel confident, capable, and ready to take on the world. But when it's low, that inner voice can turn into an inner critic, constantly pointing out your flaws and making you doubt yourself.

Everyone has an inner critic—it's that little voice in your head that loves to point out everything you think you're doing wrong. Maybe it tells you that you're not smart enough, pretty enough, or popular enough. It's like having a negative soundtrack playing in the background of your mind, and it can really drag you down if you let it.

But here's the thing: your inner critic isn't always right. In fact, it's often wrong. It tends to blow things out of proportion and focus only on the negatives while ignoring all the amazing things about you. Learning to quiet that inner critic is a big step toward building your self-esteem and confidence.

Common Causes of Low Self-Esteem

Low self-esteem doesn't just appear out of nowhere. It's often the result of a mix of experiences and feelings, like:

- Comparison:
  Constantly comparing yourself to others—especially in today's social media world—can make you feel like you're always falling short.

- Negative Experiences:

  Maybe someone said something hurtful to you, or you've gone through situations that made you feel less than. Those experiences can stick with you and impact how you see yourself.

- Perfectionism:

  If you set unrealistically high standards for yourself and then beat yourself up when you don't meet them, your self-esteem can take a hit.

- Lack of Support:

  Not having people in your life who lift you up can make it harder to feel good about yourself.

How to Build Your Confidence

The good news is, there are ways to silence that inner critic and build up your self-esteem. It's not something that happens overnight, but with practice, you can start to feel more confident and positive about who you are.

- Challenge Negative Thoughts:
  When your inner critic starts whispering negative things in your ear, challenge those thoughts. Ask yourself, "Is this really true? What evidence do I have that supports this?" Often, you'll find that your inner critic is just making stuff up. Replace those negative thoughts with more balanced, positive ones.

- Practice Self-Compassion:
  Treat yourself with the same kindness you would offer a friend. If your friend made a mistake, you wouldn't tell them they're a failure—you'd probably remind them that everyone messes up sometimes. Start giving yourself the same grace. When you're feeling down on yourself, take a moment to be kind and understanding rather than critical.

- Set Realistic Goals:
  Instead of aiming for perfection, set small, achievable goals that you can reach. Celebrate your progress, no matter how small. Each time you meet a goal, your confidence will grow a little more. Remember, building self-esteem is about progress, not perfection.

- Surround Yourself with Positive People:
  The people you spend time with have a big impact on how you feel about yourself. Try to surround yourself with friends and family who support and encourage you, rather than those who bring you down. Positive vibes are contagious, and being around uplifting people can boost your self-esteem.

- Focus on Your Strengths:
  It's easy to get caught up in what you think are your weaknesses, but don't forget about your strengths. Take some time to list out the things you're good at, whether it's a school subject, a sport, being a good friend, or anything else. Focusing on your strengths helps remind you of all the things that make you awesome.

- Step Out of Your Comfort Zone:
  Sometimes, the best way to build confidence is to push yourself to try something new, even if it's a little scary. Whether it's joining a new club, speaking up in class, or trying out for a team, taking risks can help you discover new abilities and build your confidence. And remember, even if things don't go perfectly, you're still learning and growing.

- Practice Positive Affirmations:
Positive affirmations are simple statements you can repeat to yourself to boost your confidence. Things like "I am capable," "I am enough," or "I can handle this" might feel cheesy at first, but they can actually help rewire your brain to focus on the positive. Write them down, say them out loud, or even put them on sticky notes where you'll see them every day.

- Take Care of Yourself:
Self-care is crucial for self-esteem. Make sure you're getting enough sleep, eating healthy foods, and moving your body. When you take care of your physical health, it's easier to feel good about yourself overall. Plus, feeling good physically can give you more energy and a more positive outlook.

Its time to Embrace Your True Self

Building self-esteem is a journey, not a destination. There will be ups and downs, and that's okay. What's important is that you keep moving forward, even if it's just a little bit at a time. Remember, confidence isn't about being perfect—it's about believing in yourself and knowing that you're valuable just as you are.

Your inner critic might always be there, but by practicing these strategies, you can turn down its volume and turn up the volume on your own positive, confident voice. You are enough, just as you are, and you have the power to build the confidence you need to navigate life's challenges.

So take a deep breath, stand tall, and remind yourself of this truth: You've got this.

Emotional Roller Coaster

Embracing Your Own Brushstrokes

Lily sat at her desk, staring at the half-finished painting in front of her. She had been working on it for days, but now it just looked wrong. Her art teacher's words from earlier that week echoed in her head: *"This is good, but it's not quite there yet. You need to refine your technique."*

Her technique. Lily knew she didn't paint like the other students. Her work was more abstract, more expressive, and didn't fit into the neat, realistic style her teacher preferred. But now, the criticism stung, and she started doubting herself. *Maybe I'm just not that good.*

Frustrated, she tossed her paintbrush aside and pushed the canvas away. *What's the point if I'm not even good enough for my teacher?*

The next day, Lily took a walk to clear her head. She wandered into a small art gallery near her school, hoping to find some inspiration. As she moved through the gallery, her eyes landed on a piece of art that stopped her in her tracks. It was bold, colorful, and unlike anything she had seen before. There was something raw and emotional in the brushstrokes, and it spoke to her.

"You like it?" a voice said from behind her.

Lily turned to see a woman standing beside her, smiling. "Yeah," Lily said, nodding. "It's amazing. I've never seen anything like it."

The woman chuckled softly. "Thanks. That's my painting."

Lily's eyes widened. "You painted this?"

The woman nodded. "I did. I used to go to the same school you do. Judging by your uniform, I'd guess you're a student there."

Lily blinked, still in awe. "Wow, I wish I could paint like this."

"You're an artist too?" the woman asked.

Lily hesitated. "I don't know. I mean, I try, but I don't think I'm that good. My teacher said I need to work on my technique, and now I just feel like maybe I'm not cut out for it."

The woman raised an eyebrow. "Let me guess—you feel like your style isn't good enough because it doesn't fit into what you think art should look like?"

Lily nodded. "Exactly. How did you know?"

The woman smiled knowingly. "Because I felt the same way when I was in school. I had a teacher who didn't really appreciate my style either. I doubted myself a lot, but eventually, I learned something important: self-doubt doesn't go away, even when you become a professional. What matters is how you deal with it."

Lily frowned. "But you're a professional now. Don't you feel confident in your work?"

The woman laughed. "Oh, I still feel self-doubt all the time. Every time I start a new piece, I wonder if it's going to be good enough. But I've learned to focus on what I *do* love about my work—my unique style, my colors, my vision. I remind myself of my strengths, and I keep going."

Lily thought about her own art, the way she used bold strokes and colors to express feelings she couldn't put into words. "I guess I've always liked how my paintings feel… even if they don't look perfect."

"That's a strength," the woman said, nodding. "You have something unique to offer. Not everyone will get it, and that's okay. What's important is that *you* believe in it."

Lily took a deep breath, feeling a small flicker of confidence growing inside her. "I guess I never thought about it like that."

"Try something," the woman said. "Next time you feel that self-doubt creeping in, tell yourself something positive. Remind yourself why you love creating. Focus on what makes you, *you*."

Lily smiled. "I'll try that. Thank you."

As she left the gallery, Lily felt lighter, like the weight of her teacher's criticism wasn't quite as heavy anymore. That night, she sat down at her desk, pulled her unfinished painting back in front of her, and picked up her brush. This time, she didn't worry about technique or perfection. She painted for herself, focusing on the bright, bold strokes that she loved.

And when she finished, she stood back and smiled.

Message: Everyone experiences self-doubt, even professionals. Focus on your strengths, embrace your unique style, and use positive affirmations to remind yourself of your worth as an artist. Self-doubt is natural, but it doesn't define your abilities.

Emotional Roller Coaster

Affirmation station

Select one that resonates with you each day or as needed. Feel free to repeat it as often as you like.

- I am allowed to feel all of my emotions, and they are valid.
- I am strong enough to handle difficult emotions.
- It's okay to ask for help when I need it.
- I am in control of how I respond to my feelings.
- I am worthy of love and care, no matter how I feel.
- My emotions are temporary, and they will pass.
- I trust myself to make the right choices, even when things feel overwhelming.
- I can find calm in the middle of chaos.
- Every emotion I experience teaches me more about myself.
- I deserve to take care of my mental and emotional health.
- I can create space to pause and breathe when I need it.
- I am resilient, and I can grow from challenging moments.
- I compare myself only to my highest self
- I am not trying to fit in, because I was born to stand out
- I refrain from comparing myself to others
- Beauty comes in all shapes and sizes

Emotional Roller Coaster

Chapter 5: Navigating Friendship Drama – "When BFFs Hit a Rough Patch"

Friendships can be one of the best parts of life. Your friends are the people who make you laugh, who get your weird jokes, and who are there for you when you need them. But just like any relationship, friendships can also come with their own set of challenges. Whether it's jealousy, betrayal, or just growing apart, dealing with friendship drama can be tough. But the good news is, you can work through it and come out stronger on the other side.

Jealousy – "When Green-Eyed Monsters Invade"

Jealousy is one of those emotions that can sneak up on you, even in the best of friendships. Maybe your friend got something you wanted, like a spot on the team or a higher grade, and suddenly you're feeling a little green with envy. Or maybe they've started hanging out with someone new, and you feel left out.

Jealousy can be tricky because it's not something we like to admit to ourselves, let alone to others. But it's important to remember that feeling jealous doesn't make you a bad friend—it just makes you human. The key is to handle those feelings in a healthy way, so they don't end up hurting your friendship.

How to Handle Jealousy:

- Acknowledge Your Feelings:
  The first step is to be honest with yourself. Admit that you're feeling jealous, and try to understand why. Are you worried that your friend is drifting away? Do you feel insecure about something? Understanding the root of your jealousy can help you address it.

- Talk About It:
  If jealousy is causing tension in your friendship, it might be time to have a conversation. You don't have to accuse your friend of anything—instead, try saying something like, "I've been feeling a little left out lately, and I wanted to talk to you about it." Being open about your feelings can help clear the air and prevent misunderstandings.

- Focus on Your Own Strengths:
  Instead of comparing yourself to your friend, try focusing on your own strengths and achievements. Remember that you're awesome in your own unique way, and your friend's successes don't take away from your own.

- Celebrate Your Friend's Successes:
  It might feel hard at first, but try to genuinely celebrate your friend's achievements. By being happy for them, you can turn jealousy into positivity and strengthen your friendship.

Betrayal – "When Trust Is Broken"

Betrayal is one of the hardest things to deal with in a friendship. Whether it's your friend sharing a secret you trusted them with, talking behind your back, or choosing someone else over you, betrayal can leave you feeling hurt, angry, and confused.

When trust is broken, it can feel like your whole world has been flipped upside down. But while betrayal is painful, it doesn't always mean the end of a friendship. It's possible to work through it and rebuild trust, but it takes time and effort from both sides.

How to Deal with Betrayal:

- Take Time to Process:
  It's okay to feel hurt and take some time to process what happened. You don't have to rush into making decisions about the friendship right away. Give yourself the space to feel your emotions and think about what you need.

- Communicate Honestly:
  When you're ready, talk to your friend about how you feel. Let them know how their actions affected you. It's important to be honest but also to listen to their side of the story. Sometimes, misunderstandings can lead to feelings of betrayal, and talking it out can help clear things up.

- Decide What You Need:
  After talking, think about what you need to move forward. Can you forgive your friend and rebuild trust, or do you need some distance? There's no right or wrong answer—only what feels right for you. Remember, it's okay to take a break from a friendship if you need time to heal.

- Rebuild Trust Slowly:
  If you decide to work on the friendship, rebuilding trust takes time. It's important for both of you to be patient and show through your actions that you're committed to making things right. It won't happen overnight, but with time, it's possible to heal.

Growing Apart – "When You're Not on the Same Page Anymore"

Sometimes, friendships don't end with a big fight or betrayal—they just fade. You and your friend might start drifting apart, maybe because of different interests, new friend groups, or just growing up. Growing apart can be tough because it's often nobody's fault, but it can still leave you feeling lonely and confused.

Growing apart doesn't mean you have to stop being friends, but it might mean that your friendship changes. And that's okay. People grow and change, and sometimes friendships need to adapt to those changes.

How to Handle Growing Apart:

- Acknowledge the Change:

It's okay to admit that things are different. Maybe you don't hang out as much, or you don't feel as close as you used to. Acknowledging that things have changed can help you figure out what you want from the friendship moving forward.

- Talk to Your Friend:
  If you're feeling sad about growing apart, talk to your friend about it. You might find that they're feeling the same way. Together, you can decide how to move forward, whether that means making an effort to reconnect or accepting that your friendship is evolving.

- Focus on What You Still Have:
  Even if you're not as close as you used to be, that doesn't mean your friendship isn't valuable. Focus on the positive aspects of your relationship and appreciate the memories you've shared. You can still care about each other, even if your friendship looks different now.

- Be Open to New Friendships:
  As you grow and change, it's natural to make new friends who share your current interests and values. Don't be afraid to open yourself up to new connections, while still cherishing the friendships you've had.

There will be Ups and Downs of Friendship

Friendships, like any relationship, have their ups and downs. Whether you're dealing with jealousy, betrayal, or just growing apart, it's important to remember that these challenges are a normal part of life. They don't mean you're a bad friend, and they don't mean your friendship is doomed.

By facing these issues head-on, communicating openly, and being patient with yourself and your friends, you can navigate even the roughest patches. And through it all, you'll learn more about yourself, your friends, and what it means to be a true friend.

So, the next time friendship drama pops up, take a deep breath and remember—you've got the tools to handle it, and you're stronger than you think.

Emotional Roller Coaster

Growing in New Directions

Sofia scrolled through her phone, her heart sinking as she saw the photos. Her friends—Mia, Harper, and Olivia—had gone to the movies without her. Again. They had posted pictures, all smiling and laughing, while Sofia sat at home wondering why she hadn't been invited.

What did I do wrong? she thought, her chest tightening. It wasn't the first time she had felt left out, and each time it happened, it hurt a little more. These were the friends she'd grown up with, the ones who knew everything about her. But lately, it felt like they were drifting away, like they didn't need her anymore.

She threw her phone down on her bed and stared at the ceiling, feeling a lump in her throat. *What if they don't like me anymore?*

The next day at school, Sofia couldn't focus. During lunch, Mia and the others sat together, laughing like nothing was wrong, but Sofia didn't feel like joining them. She sat at the edge of the table, picking at her food, her mind racing with questions. Should she say something? Should she just let it go?

That afternoon, as she walked home from school, Sofia ran into her neighbor, Ms. Jenkins, who was outside tending to her garden. Ms. Jenkins smiled warmly as Sofia approached.

"Hey, Sofia. You look like you've got a lot on your mind. Want to talk about it?"

Sofia hesitated, but something about Ms. Jenkins' kind smile made her feel comfortable. "It's just... my friends," she began slowly. "They've been hanging out without me a lot lately, and I don't know why. I feel like they don't want to be friends anymore."

Ms. Jenkins nodded, listening carefully. "That sounds really tough. It's hard when you feel like you're being left out."

Sofia sighed. "Yeah, it is. I don't want to lose them, but I don't know what to do."

Ms. Jenkins thought for a moment before saying, "You know, friendships change as we grow. Sometimes people drift apart, and sometimes they come back together. It's normal for things to shift, especially as everyone starts finding new interests or spending time with different people."

Sofia frowned. "But what if they don't want to be friends with me anymore?"

"Well," Ms. Jenkins said gently, "Have you talked to them about how you feel?"

Sofia shook her head. "No, I'm scared it'll just make things worse."

Ms. Jenkins smiled kindly. "I know it can be scary to talk about your feelings, but communication is really important in any relationship. Your friends might not even realize they've been leaving you out. Sometimes, people just get caught up in their own lives without meaning to hurt anyone."

Sofia bit her lip, thinking about what Ms. Jenkins said. She had never really considered that her friends might not be doing this on purpose.

Ms. Jenkins continued, "And you know, it's also okay to branch out and meet new people. Friendships don't have to end; they just evolve. You can still be close to your old friends while also making new ones. Sometimes, meeting new people helps you grow in ways you didn't expect."

That night, after thinking over what Ms. Jenkins said, Sofia decided to be brave. She texted Mia: *Hey, can we talk? I've been feeling a little left out lately, and I just want to know if everything's okay between us.*

Mia replied almost immediately: *Oh no, Sofia, I'm so sorry! We didn't mean to make you feel left out. We've just been really busy with soccer and stuff. Let's all hang out this weekend, okay?*

Relief washed over Sofia. Maybe Ms. Jenkins was right—sometimes, people just don't realize how their actions affect others.

That weekend, Sofia joined her friends for a movie, and things felt almost back to normal. But as the days went on, she also found herself talking to new people in her art class and during lunch. Slowly, she started to branch out, meeting new friends who shared her interests. It didn't mean she loved Mia, Harper, and Olivia any less—it just meant her world was growing.

As Sofia sat in art class, laughing with her new friend, Grace, she realized that friendships didn't have to stay the same to be important. They could change, and that was okay. She was changing too.

Message: Friendships evolve over time, and it's okay to branch out and meet new people. Communication is key when resolving conflicts with friends, and it's important to talk about your feelings. Friendships don't have to end; they can grow in new directions.

Emotional Roller Coaster

Chapter 6: Understanding Anger – "It's Okay to Be Mad"

Anger. It's that fiery feeling that can come out of nowhere and take over your whole body. Your heart races, your muscles tense, and you might feel like you're about to explode. Whether it's because someone said something hurtful, you're dealing with a frustrating situation, or things just aren't going your way, anger is a powerful emotion. But here's the thing: anger isn't bad. It's a normal, natural emotion that everyone feels from time to time.

The important part isn't whether you get angry—it's how you handle that anger. When anger is expressed in healthy ways, it can actually be a positive force. But when it's bottled up or comes out in harmful ways, it can hurt you and those around you. Let's talk about how to understand your anger and find healthy ways to express it.

Why Do We Get Angry?

Anger usually pops up when we feel like something is unfair, when we're being treated badly, or when things aren't going the way we want. It's our body's way of telling us that something is wrong and that we need to do something about it. In a way, anger is like a big red flag waving in your face, saying, "Hey, pay attention! Something's not right here!"

There are lots of things that can trigger anger. Maybe someone cut in front of you in line, or a friend made a joke that hurt your feelings. Maybe you're frustrated because you're struggling with schoolwork, or you feel like no one's listening to you. Whatever the reason, it's important to remember that feeling angry is okay. It's what you do with that anger that matters.

Healthy Ways to Express Anger

When you're angry, it can be tempting to lash out—yell at someone, throw something, or say something you don't mean. But while those reactions might feel good in the moment, they usually just make things worse. Instead, there are healthier ways to express your anger that can help you feel better without causing harm.

- Pause and Breathe:
  When you feel anger bubbling up, take a moment to pause and breathe. It might sound simple, but taking a few deep breaths can help calm your body and mind, giving you a chance to think before you react. Try breathing in slowly for a count of four, holding your breath for a moment, and then exhaling for another count of four.

- Identify What You're Really Feeling:
  Sometimes, anger is a mask for other emotions, like hurt, embarrassment, or fear. Take a moment to ask yourself what's really going on underneath your anger. Are you feeling left out? Are you scared of something? Understanding the root cause of your anger can help you figure out the best way to address it.

- Use "I" Statements:
  If you need to talk to someone about what's making you angry, try using "I" statements. Instead of saying, "You're so annoying!" try saying, "I feel really frustrated when you interrupt me." This way, you're expressing your feelings without blaming or attacking the other person, which can help keep the conversation calm and productive.

- Find a Healthy Outlet:
  Sometimes, you just need to release your anger in a physical way. Find a healthy outlet that works for you—go for a run, hit a pillow, or even just scream into a pillow. Physical activity can help burn off some of that angry energy and clear your mind.

- Write It Out:
  If you're not ready to talk about your anger, try writing it down instead. Journaling about what's making you mad can help you process your feelings and get some clarity on the situation. You might find that once it's on paper, your anger doesn't feel quite as overwhelming.

- Take a Break:
  If you're in a situation where you're feeling really angry, it's okay to take a break. Walk away from the situation for a little while to cool down. Taking a break doesn't mean you're avoiding the issue—it just means you're giving yourself time to calm down so you can deal with it more effectively later.

- Talk to Someone You Trust:
  Sometimes, just talking to someone you trust can help you process your anger. Whether it's a friend, family member, or

counselor, having someone listen to you can help you feel heard and supported.

They might even be able to offer advice or a different perspective on the situation.

When Anger Gets Out of Control

While anger is a natural emotion, sometimes it can feel like it's taking over your life. If you find yourself getting angry all the time, or if your anger is leading to hurtful actions or strained relationships, it might be a sign that you need some extra help. Talking to a counselor or therapist can help you learn new ways to manage your anger and find healthier ways to express it.

Embracing Your Anger in a Healthy Way

Anger isn't something to be afraid of or ashamed of—it's just another part of being human. By understanding your anger and finding healthy ways to express it, you can turn it into a positive force in your life. Whether it's standing up for yourself, setting boundaries, or addressing a problem, your anger can be a powerful tool for making things better.

Remember, it's okay to be mad. What's important is how you choose to deal with that anger. So the next time you feel your temper rising, take a deep breath, listen to what your anger is telling you, and find a way to express it that helps rather than hurts. You've got the strength to handle it.

Finding a Way to Let It Out

Kayla stormed into the house, slamming her backpack onto the floor. It had been one of those days—nothing had gone right. She'd failed her math test, forgotten her homework, and had an argument with her best friend. As she kicked off her shoes, her little brother, Jacob, ran up to her, waving a toy in her face.

"Kayla, look! Look at what I made!" he exclaimed, his eyes wide with excitement.

"Not now, Jacob!" Kayla snapped, her voice louder than she intended. "I don't care about your dumb toy!"

Jacob's face fell, and he quickly retreated to his room without saying another word. The guilt hit Kayla immediately, but she was too frustrated to apologize. She didn't mean to lash out at him, but the anger bubbling inside her needed somewhere to go. She sat on the couch, burying her face in her hands. *Why do I always do this?*

Emotional Roller Coaster

Later that afternoon, Kayla had soccer practice. As soon as she hit the field, she started kicking the ball with all her might, taking out her frustration on the grass and the net. Her coach, Coach Davis, noticed her intensity and called her over after practice.

"Kayla, you've been playing with a lot of fire today," Coach Davis said, raising an eyebrow. "Something bothering you?"

Kayla shrugged, unsure of what to say. "I just had a bad day, I guess."

Coach Davis nodded, as if she understood exactly what Kayla meant. "You know, I've had plenty of bad days too. But I've learned that physical activity—like running or playing soccer—can be a great way to release those emotions."

Kayla looked down at her cleats. "Yeah, I guess. But I still feel bad. I yelled at my little brother for no reason."

Coach Davis smiled softly. "We all lose our temper sometimes, especially when we're upset about something else. But there are healthier ways to handle it. Physical outlets like sports or even creative activities can help get that anger out without hurting others."

Kayla nodded, thinking about how good it had felt to kick the ball hard during practice. "I didn't mean to take it out on him. I just—everything went wrong today."

"I get it," Coach Davis said. "When you feel anger building up, try to recognize it before it spills over. You can go for a run, write about how you're feeling, or even just talk to someone. It's important to express your feelings with words rather than actions that you might regret later."

Kayla thought about it for a moment. "I think I need to apologize to Jacob."

"That's a good start," Coach Davis said, smiling. "And remember, next time you feel like you're about to lose it, find a way to let it out in a way that helps you, not hurts others."

When Kayla got home, she found Jacob playing quietly in his room. She knocked on the door and stepped inside.

"Hey, Jacob," she said softly, feeling her stomach twist with guilt. "I'm sorry for yelling at you earlier. I didn't mean it. I just had a really tough day."

Jacob looked up at her, his eyes wide. "It's okay. Do you want to see the toy I made now?"

Kayla smiled and nodded. "Yeah, I'd love to."

As Jacob excitedly showed her his creation, Kayla realized that Coach Davis was right—channeling her anger into something positive made all the difference. And while she couldn't undo what had happened earlier, she could try to handle her emotions better next time.

Message: Physical outlets like exercise and creative activities can help release anger in a healthy way. Expressing anger with words, instead of hurtful actions, helps maintain relationships and allows for growth. It's okay to feel angry, but it's important to channel that emotion constructively.

The Anger Reflection and Action Plan

Objective: To help understand your anger triggers, explore healthy ways to express and manage anger, and create a personal action plan for dealing with anger.

Materials Needed:
- Journal or notebook
- Pen or pencil
- Optional: Colored markers or pencils for visual representation

Instructions:

1. *Reflect on Your Anger Triggers*:
Think about recent situations where you felt angry. List these situations and describe what triggered your anger.

    Example prompts:
- What happened to make you feel angry?
- How did you react at the moment?
- How did your reaction affect the situation and the people involved?

2. *Identify Patterns and Feelings:*

Reflect on common patterns in their anger responses. Write about what tends to trigger your anger and how you usually express it.

Example prompts:
- Do you notice any common themes or patterns in what makes you angry?
- How do you typically express your anger (e.g., shouting, withdrawing, frustration)?
- How does your anger affect your relationships and your well-being?

3. *Explore Healthy Anger Management Strategies:*

Provide a list of healthy ways to manage and express anger, such as:
- Deep breathing exercises
- Physical activities like jogging or yoga
- Creative outlets like drawing or writing
- Talking to someone you trust

Choose a few strategies you think would work for you and write about how you could implement these strategies in your life.

4. *Create an Action Plan:*

Develop a personal action plan for managing anger. You should outline specific steps you will take when you start to feel angry.

Example prompts:
- What are your go-to strategies for calming down when you're angry?
- How will you remind yourself to use these strategies in the heat of the moment?
- What are some alternative ways to express your anger constructively?

5. *Visual Representation (Optional):*
- If using colored markers or pencils, create a visual representation of your anger triggers and coping strategies. You can create a chart, mind map, or even a visual journal page that illustrates your thoughts and plans.

Be sure to revisit your action plans regularly and reflect on your progress. Understanding and managing anger is an ongoing process, and it's okay to seek help if needed.

Emotional Roller Coaster

Chapter 7: First Crushes and Romantic Rollercoasters – "Is This What Love Feels Like?"

Crushes—they can hit you out of nowhere. One day, you're just going about your life, and the next, you can't stop thinking about that one person. Maybe it's the way they smile, the way they laugh, or just the way they make you feel when they're around. Suddenly, your heart races when you see them, and you feel a little nervous, excited, and maybe even a bit confused. Welcome to the world of first crushes and infatuation.

Crushes are one of those experiences almost everyone goes through, and they can be a mix of thrilling, overwhelming, and sometimes even painful emotions. Whether it's your first crush or one of many, navigating these feelings can be tricky. But it's all part of growing up and figuring out what love and relationships mean to you.

The Excitement of a First Crush

Having a crush can be one of the most exciting feelings in the world. Suddenly, everything about that person seems amazing, and you can't wait to see them or even just catch a glimpse of them in the hallway.

You might find yourself daydreaming about them, wondering what it would be like if they liked you back. It's easy to get lost in these thoughts and feelings, and that's totally normal.

Why Crushes Feel So Intense:

- New Emotions:
  If it's your first crush, these feelings might be brand new to you, which can make them feel even more intense. Your brain is releasing all kinds of chemicals like dopamine, which makes you feel happy and excited whenever you think about your crush.

- Imagination at Work:
  Crushes often involve a lot of imagination. You might picture what it would be like to hang out with them, go on dates, or just spend time together. This daydreaming can make your feelings even stronger because you're creating a whole world in your mind where everything is perfect.

- The Thrill of the Unknown:
  Part of what makes crushes so powerful is that they're full of possibility. You don't know what could happen—maybe they like you back, maybe they don't, but the mystery is part of the thrill.

Infatuation vs. Real Connection

When you have a crush, it can be easy to get swept up in the excitement and start thinking about your crush as the most amazing person ever. But it's important to remember that crushes are often based on infatuation—an intense but short-lived passion for someone. Infatuation can feel a lot like love, but it's usually more about the idea of the person than who they really are.

Infatuation is usually:

- Focused on Appearances:
  You might be drawn to how someone looks, dresses, or carries themselves. You're attracted to the surface-level things, which can make your feelings intense but also a little shallow.

- All-Consuming:
  When you're infatuated, it can feel like you can't think about anything else. Your crush might be on your mind constantly, and you might find yourself obsessing over little things they do or say.

- Quick to Start, Quick to Fade:
  Infatuation can come on strong, but it can also fade quickly, especially if you start to see the person's flaws or realize that you don't have as much in common as you thought.

Real Connection is:

- Built on Knowing the Person:
  A real connection goes deeper than looks. It's about knowing the person's personality, values, and interests and liking them for who they are, not just how they appear.

- Mutual Respect and Understanding:
  In a real connection, both people respect and understand each other. It's not just about the

excitement of a crush—it's about genuinely caring for each other.

- *Developed Over Time:*
  Unlike infatuation, which can happen almost instantly, real connections take time to build. They grow as you get to know each other better and spend more time together.

The Ups and Downs of Romantic Feelings

Romantic feelings can be a wild ride. One minute, you're on cloud nine because your crush smiled at you, and the next, you're feeling down because they didn't notice you in the hallway. These emotional ups and downs are totally normal, but they can be hard to handle.

- *Dealing with Rejection:*
  One of the toughest parts of having a crush is the possibility of rejection. Maybe your crush doesn't like you back, or they might even be interested in someone else. Rejection can sting, but it's important to remember that it doesn't mean there's anything wrong

with you. It just means that this person isn't the right match for you, and that's okay. There are plenty of other people out there, and one rejection doesn't define your worth.

- *Navigating the Crush:*
  If you think your crush might like you back, it can be both exciting and nerve-wracking. You might wonder how to make the first move, or whether you should even try. If you decide to tell them how you feel, it can be scary, but it can also be a great way to see if there's a real connection between you two. Remember, it's okay to take things slow and just enjoy the process of getting to know someone better.

- *When Things Don't Work Out:*
  Sometimes, crushes don't turn into anything more, and that can be disappointing. It's natural to feel sad or frustrated when things don't go the way you hoped, but it's also a chance to learn and grow. Every experience, even the ones that don't work out, teaches you something about yourself and what you want in a relationship.

Keeping Perspective

While crushes can feel like the most important thing in the world, it's important to keep perspective. Remember that your life is full of other things that matter—your friends, your family, your hobbies, and your goals. It's great to have a crush, but don't let it take over your life. Stay true to yourself and keep doing the things that make you happy.

Just enjoy the Ride

First crushes and the ups and downs of romantic feelings are a normal part of growing up. They can be exciting, confusing, and sometimes even a little painful, but they're also a chance to learn more about yourself and what you want in a relationship. So, enjoy the ride, keep an open heart, and remember—you're just beginning to explore the world of love and relationships, and there's so much more to discover.

Whether your crush turns into something more or just stays a fun memory, every experience helps you grow. And who knows? The next crush might just be the start of something amazing.

Emotional Roller Coaster

Beyond the Crush

Naomi's heart skipped a beat every time she saw Ethan in the hallway. His laugh, his style, even the way he brushed his hair off his forehead—it all made her feel like she was on an emotional rollercoaster. One moment, she would be elated just thinking about him, and the next, she'd be spiraling into self-doubt, wondering if he even knew she existed.

Her friends noticed how distracted she was lately. Naomi found it hard to focus on her schoolwork, and even during lunch, she barely joined in on conversations. Her thoughts were consumed by Ethan, and she felt overwhelmed by the intensity of her feelings.

One evening, Naomi sat at the kitchen table, struggling with her homework. Her older sister, Jess, walked in and saw the frustrated look on Naomi's face.

"Hey, you've been in a funk lately," Jess said, sitting down next to her. "What's going on?"

Naomi hesitated before admitting, "I've got this huge crush on Ethan, and it's driving me crazy. I can't stop thinking about him, and it's making everything else seem so unimportant."

Jess raised an eyebrow, a knowing smile tugging at her lips. "Ah, crushes. They can be pretty intense, can't they? What's been the hardest part?"

Naomi sighed. "It's just... one minute, I'm excited and daydreaming about him, and the next, I'm convinced he doesn't even notice me. It feels like my whole mood depends on what's happening with him."

Jess nodded sympathetically. "Crushes can feel like the center of your world, but it's important to remember that they're just one part of it. They don't define your worth. Just because you have feelings for someone doesn't mean your value is tied to their response."

Naomi frowned, feeling a pang of guilt. "But it's hard not to feel like it does. I just keep thinking, 'What if he never notices me? What if this is all for nothing?'"

Jess put a comforting hand on Naomi's shoulder. "I get it. But think about it this way: you're a whole person on your own. Your self-worth isn't dependent on someone else's approval. It's great to have feelings for someone, but it's also important to maintain your own identity and remember that you're awesome just as you are."

Naomi looked thoughtful. "So, you're saying I should focus on myself, not just on him?"

"Exactly," Jess said with a warm smile. "When you invest in yourself, your interests, and your passions, you become more confident and happier. And guess what? That confidence can make you even more appealing to others. But even if Ethan never notices you in the way you hope, it doesn't change how incredible you are."

Naomi's shoulders relaxed a bit. "Thanks, Jess. I guess I needed to hear that. It's hard to remember sometimes."

Jess nodded. "It really is. But remember, crushes come and go, and your worth is constant. Take care of yourself, enjoy your hobbies, and don't let your feelings for Ethan overshadow all the amazing things about you."

Feeling a bit lighter, Naomi decided to focus on her favorite activities—painting and hanging out with friends—without letting

Ethan's presence dominate her thoughts. She realized that while having a crush was exciting, it wasn't the only thing that defined her.

As days passed, Naomi found that her mood stabilized. She still liked Ethan, but she no longer felt like her entire happiness hinged on him. Instead, she embraced her own interests and let her self-confidence grow. And who knew? Maybe Ethan would notice her, or maybe he wouldn't, but either way, Naomi knew she was enough just as she was.

Message: Crushes are a normal part of life, but they don't define your worth. It's important to maintain your own identity and self-love in relationships. Focus on your own interests and well-being, and remember that your value isn't tied to someone else's response.

Chapter 8: Finding Joy in the Little Things – *"Bright Spots in Tough Times"*

Life isn't always easy. Sometimes, things don't go the way we want, and it can feel like everything is just too much to handle. Maybe you're dealing with stress at school, a fight with a friend, or just a general feeling of being overwhelmed. During these tough times, it's easy to get caught up in the negative and forget about the good things that are still happening all around you. But here's the thing: even on the hardest days, there are moments of joy and happiness waiting to be noticed—you just have to look for them.

Finding joy in the little things doesn't mean ignoring the challenges you're facing. It's about recognizing that even in the middle of difficulties, there are bright spots that can lift your spirits and remind you that life is full of moments worth appreciating.

The Power of Small Moments

We often think that happiness comes from big events—getting a good grade, winning a game, or going on a fun trip. But the truth is, some of the most meaningful and lasting happiness comes from the small, everyday moments. These are the things that can easily go unnoticed, but when you start paying attention, you realize how much joy they can bring.

Examples of Small Moments to Cherish:

- A Warm Sunrise:
  There's something magical about watching the sky light up with colors in the early morning. It's a reminder that every day is a new beginning, full of possibilities.

- A Favorite Song on the Radio:
  When your favorite song comes on unexpectedly, it can instantly brighten your mood. Sing along, dance a little, and let the music fill you with happiness.

- A Kind Word from a Friend:
  A simple compliment or a word of encouragement from a friend can make a big difference in your day. It's a reminder that you're cared for and appreciated.

- A Quiet Moment with a Pet:
  If you have a pet, you know how comforting it can be to spend a few quiet minutes cuddling with them. Their unconditional love is one of life's greatest joys.

- The Smell of Freshly Baked Cookies:
  Sometimes, joy is as simple as a delicious smell wafting through the house. Take a moment to savor it and enjoy the simple pleasure of a treat.

Why Finding Joy Matters

When you're going through a tough time, it can be hard to see the good in anything. But finding joy in the small things is a powerful way to shift your focus and remind yourself that life isn't all bad. These little moments of happiness can give you the strength to keep going, even when things are tough.

- *Building Resilience:*
  Resilience is the ability to bounce back from challenges and keep moving forward. When you make a habit of finding joy in small moments, you're building resilience. You're training your brain to notice the positive, even

when life is difficult, which can help you stay strong and hopeful.

- *Reducing Stress:*
  Focusing on the small joys in life can help reduce stress. When you take a moment to appreciate something simple, like a beautiful flower or a funny joke, your body and mind get a break from the stress and worry. It's like hitting the pause button on your problems, even if it's just for a few seconds.

- *Improving Your Mood:*
  Small moments of joy can have a big impact on your overall mood. Even if you're feeling down, finding something to smile about—even something small—can help lift your spirits. Over time, these little boosts can add up, helping you feel more positive and hopeful.

How to Find Joy When Things Feel Tough

When life is hard, finding joy might not come naturally. It's something you have to practice, like building a muscle. Here are some ways to start noticing and appreciating the small moments of joy in your life:

- Keep a Gratitude Journal:
Each day, write down three things that made you smile or feel good. They don't have to be big things—just anything that brought you a little bit of joy. Over time, you'll start to notice more and more things to be grateful for.

- Slow Down and Notice:
In our busy lives, it's easy to rush through the day without noticing the small things. Make an effort to slow down and pay attention. Whether it's the sound of birds chirping or the feeling of the sun on your face, take a moment to really experience and appreciate it.

- Celebrate Small Wins:
Did you finish a difficult homework assignment? Make it to the bus on time? Remember to text a friend back? These might seem like small accomplishments, but they're worth celebrating. Give yourself credit for the little things you do right.

- Practice Mindfulness:
Mindfulness is all about being present in the moment. Try to focus on what you're doing right now, rather than

worrying about the past or the future. When you're mindful, you're more likely to notice and appreciate the small joys that are all around you.

- Share the Joy:
Sometimes, joy is even better when it's shared. If something makes you happy, share it with a friend or family member. Whether it's a funny meme or a beautiful sunset, sharing the moment can double the joy.

Embracing Life's Bright Spots

Life will always have its ups and downs, but by focusing on the bright spots—the small moments of joy—you can make the tough times a little easier to bear. These moments won't solve all your problems, but they can remind you that there's still good in the world, even when things are hard.

So, the next time you're feeling overwhelmed, take a deep breath and look around. What's one small thing you can appreciate right now? Maybe it's the way your dog wags its tail when you walk in the room, or the way your favorite snack tastes just right. Whatever it is, take a moment to savor it. These little joys are life's way of reminding you that there's always something to smile about, even on the toughest days.

Emotional Roller Coaster

The Simple Joy of Helping Out

Mia trudged home from school, feeling weighed down by the events of the past week. It had been tough—exams, arguments with friends, and a general sense of things not going her way. Everything seemed to be going wrong, and Mia couldn't shake the feeling of gloom that had settled over her.

As she approached her house, she noticed her elderly neighbor, Mr. Thompson, struggling with a small garden project. He was trying to set up a birdhouse but seemed to be having trouble.

Mia hesitated for a moment. She was exhausted and in no mood for extra tasks, but something about Mr. Thompson's determined expression made her pause. He looked up and saw her standing there.

"Hi, Mia," Mr. Thompson said with a warm smile. "Could you give me a hand with this birdhouse? I'm afraid I'm not as steady as I used to be."

Mia shrugged, her curiosity piqued despite her mood. "Sure, Mr. Thompson. What do you need help with?"

Together, they worked on the birdhouse. Mia measured and sawed while Mr. Thompson guided her, sharing stories about his own childhood projects. Despite her initial reluctance, Mia found herself enjoying the task. There was something satisfying about working with her hands and seeing the birdhouse take shape.

As they worked, Mr. Thompson chatted about his love for birds and how the birdhouse would provide a cozy home for them. His enthusiasm was contagious, and Mia started to feel a sense of accomplishment. She was helping someone, and it felt good.

When they finished, Mr. Thompson beamed with pride. "Thank you, Mia. I couldn't have done this without you."

Mia smiled back, feeling a surprising warmth in her chest. "It was actually kind of fun. Thanks for letting me help."

Later that evening, Mia sat at her desk, reflecting on her day. She realized that despite the rough week, helping Mr. Thompson had brought a sense of joy she hadn't expected. It was a small moment, but it had made her feel better.

She decided to keep a gratitude journal, jotting down little things that made her smile each day. From the satisfaction of completing the birdhouse to the smile Mr. Thompson had given her, she started to see the beauty in everyday moments.

Mia found that focusing on these small, positive experiences helped shift her perspective. Her week was still challenging, but she discovered that joy could come from simple things—like helping a neighbor and finding purpose in unexpected places.

Message: Joy can be found in simple, everyday moments. Helping others and focusing on small acts of kindness can boost your mood and provide a sense of fulfillment. Gratitude for these small moments can shift your perspective and bring unexpected happiness.

Emotional Roller Coaster

Chapter 9: The Power of Self-Reflection – "Getting to Know Your Emotions"

Emotions are a big part of life, especially during your teen years when everything seems to be changing so fast. You might feel like you're on an emotional rollercoaster, with ups and downs that are hard to predict or control. But here's the good news: you have the power to understand and manage your emotions better through self-reflection.

Self-reflection is like holding up a mirror to your inner world. It's about taking the time to really think about what you're feeling, why you're feeling it, and how those feelings are affecting your thoughts and actions. When you make self-reflection a regular habit, you start to get to know yourself better. You can identify patterns in your emotions, understand what triggers them, and figure out the best ways to cope.

Why Self-Reflection Matters

In the rush of everyday life, it's easy to get swept up in your emotions without really understanding them. You might find yourself reacting without thinking, or feeling overwhelmed by emotions that seem to come out of nowhere. Self-reflection helps you slow down and make sense of what's going on inside you.

Benefits of Self-Reflection:

- Understanding Triggers:
  By reflecting on your emotions, you can start to identify what triggers certain feelings. Maybe you notice that you always feel anxious before a big test, or that you get frustrated when plans change unexpectedly. Once you know your triggers, you can work on strategies to manage them.

- Gaining Perspective:
  When you take a step back and reflect, you can see your emotions from a different perspective. This can help you realize that feelings are temporary and that you have the ability to choose how you respond to them.

- Improving Decision-Making:
Emotions can cloud your judgment and lead to impulsive decisions. Self-reflection helps you pause and consider your options before reacting, leading to better choices and fewer regrets.

- Building Emotional Intelligence:
Emotional intelligence is the ability to recognize, understand, and manage your own emotions, as well as the emotions of others. Self-reflection is a key part of developing emotional intelligence, which is an important skill for building healthy relationships and navigating life's challenges.

How to Practice Self-Reflection

Self-reflection doesn't have to be complicated. It's something you can do anytime, anywhere—whether you're sitting quietly in your room, taking a walk, or just lying in bed before falling asleep. The key is to make it a regular habit, so it becomes a natural part of your routine.

Steps to Start Self-Reflecting:

- Find a Quiet Space:
  It's easier to reflect when you're in a calm, quiet environment. Find a spot where you won't be interrupted, and take a few deep breaths to relax your mind.

- Ask Yourself Questions:
  Self-reflection starts with asking yourself the right questions. Here are a few to get you started:
    - What am I feeling right now?
    - What happened that might have caused this emotion?
    - How did I react to this emotion? Was it helpful or harmful?
    - What could I do differently next time?

- Write It Down:
  Journaling is a great way to reflect on your emotions. Writing things down can help you organize your thoughts and see patterns that you might not notice otherwise. Try keeping a journal where you jot down

your feelings, what triggered them, and how you responded.

- Be Honest with Yourself:
Self-reflection only works if you're honest with yourself. It's okay to admit when you're struggling or when you've made a mistake. The goal isn't to judge yourself but to learn and grow.

- Look for Patterns:
Over time, you'll start to notice patterns in your emotions. Maybe you always feel sad on Sunday nights, or you get angry when you're hungry. Recognizing these patterns can help you prepare and manage your emotions better.

- Practice Self-Compassion:
As you reflect, it's important to be kind to yourself. Everyone has difficult emotions and moments they're not proud of. Instead of being hard on yourself, practice self-compassion. Remind yourself that it's okay to have feelings and that you're doing your best to manage them.

-

- Set Intentions for the Future:
Self-reflection isn't just about looking back—it's also about moving forward. After reflecting on your emotions, set intentions for how you want to handle similar situations in the future. This might mean deciding to take deep breaths when you're angry, or to reach out to a friend when you're feeling down.

The Benefits of Knowing Yourself

The more you practice self-reflection, the better you'll get at understanding your emotions. You'll start to notice patterns, recognize triggers, and develop strategies that help you stay calm and in control. This kind of self-awareness is incredibly empowering. It gives you the tools to manage your emotions in a healthy way, rather than letting them control you.

Self-reflection also helps you build a stronger sense of self. When you know yourself better, you're more confident in your decisions and more resilient in the face of challenges. You learn to trust your instincts and rely on your inner strength, which can make a big difference when life gets tough.

Embrace the Journey

Self-reflection is a journey, not a destination. It's something you'll continue to do throughout your life as you grow and change. The more you practice, the more you'll learn about yourself and your emotions. And the more you understand your emotions, the better equipped you'll be to navigate the ups and downs of life.

So, the next time you're feeling overwhelmed, take a moment to pause and reflect. Ask yourself what you're feeling and why. Write it down, if that helps. And remember, it's okay to feel whatever you're feeling. By taking the time to understand your emotions, you're taking a powerful step toward managing them and living a more balanced, fulfilling life.

Emotional Roller Coaster

Reflections of Growth

Victoria sat on her bed, surrounded by the soft glow of her desk lamp, flipping through the pages of her journal. It had been a year filled with ups and downs, and she wanted to take a moment to reflect. She had started journaling as a way to manage her stress, but tonight, she was looking back at everything she had written.

As she read through her entries, Victoria remembered the highs—the excitement of making the varsity soccer team, the joy of her best friend's surprise birthday party, and the thrill of getting accepted into the summer internship program she had dreamed about. Each of these moments was recorded in bright, hopeful colors in her journal.

But there were also lows—struggles with a challenging class, a fallout with a close friend, and the disappointment of not achieving a goal she had worked so hard for. These moments were marked by frustration and sadness, but as Victoria reread them, she saw how she had faced each challenge with resilience.

In her journal, she had detailed not just the events, but her feelings and the lessons she had learned from them. Reflecting on her past struggles, she saw how she had grown emotionally. She had developed a better understanding of herself and learned to handle her emotions with more grace. What had once felt overwhelming now seemed like a series of valuable learning experiences.

Victoria paused at a recent entry where she had written about a particularly tough period. She had felt lost and unsure, but the entry ended with a note of hope and a plan for how to approach similar challenges in the future. Reading that now, she realized how far she had come.

She closed her journal and took a deep breath, feeling a newfound sense of confidence. The challenges of the past year had taught her valuable lessons about herself and her ability to overcome difficulties. She knew that while the future would bring new obstacles, she was better equipped to handle them with the resilience and self-awareness she had gained.

With this realization, Victoria felt ready to face whatever came next. She understood that journaling had not only been a way to process her feelings but also a tool for growth. By reflecting on her experiences, she had learned to approach future challenges with greater confidence and optimism.

Message: Journaling is a powerful tool for self-reflection and emotional growth. By looking back on past experiences, you can gain insight into how you've grown and learn how to approach future challenges with greater confidence.

Emotional Roller Coaster

Reflecting

Here are some journal prompts to help you reflect on your growth and approach future challenges with confidence:

1. ***Reflect on Growth***:
    - What are three significant challenges you've faced this year? How did you overcome them, and what did you learn from each experience?

    _____
    _____
    _____
    _____

    - What are some moments or accomplishments from the past year that you're particularly proud of? How did these achievements make you feel about yourself?

    _____
    _____
    _____
    _____

2. ***Emotional Lessons:***
    - How have your emotional responses to challenges changed over the past year? What strategies have you developed to handle difficult emotions?

    _____
    _____
    _____
    _____

    - Can you recall a time when you felt overwhelmed by a situation? How did you manage to get through it, and what would you do differently now?

    _____
    _____
    _____
    _____

3. ***Self-Awareness:***
    - In what ways have you grown emotionally and personally this year? How do you think these changes have shaped who you are today?

    _____
    _____

- How has your understanding of yourself and your strengths evolved over the past year? What new insights have you gained about your abilities?

4. ***Future Outlook:***
    - Looking ahead, what challenges do you anticipate facing in the next year? How can you apply the lessons you've learned to approach these challenges with confidence?

-

- What personal goals or aspirations do you have for the coming year? How can you use your past experiences to help you achieve these goals?

_____
_____
_____
_____

5. **_Gratitude and Reflection:_**
- What are three things you're grateful for from the past year? How have these things impacted your life and your outlook?

_____
_____
_____
_____

- Reflect on a time when someone offered you support or guidance. How did their help influence your ability to handle a difficult situation?

_____
_____

6. ***Self-Care and Resilience:***
- How have you practiced self-care during tough times this year? What self-care strategies have worked best for you?

- What are some positive affirmations or mantras that have helped you through challenging moments? How can you remind yourself of these in the future?

Emotional Roller Coaster

Chapter 10: Embracing the Full Spectrum – "All Your Emotions Belong"

As we come to the end of this journey together, there's one final message I want to leave you with: all your emotions belong. Every feeling you've ever had, from the highest highs to the lowest lows, is a part of what makes you, you. Life is a wild, unpredictable ride, and emotions are like the colors that paint your experience. Some days, the colors are bright and vibrant; other days, they're darker and more subdued. But every shade has its place and its purpose.

The Beauty of Being Human

To be human is to feel. It's what makes us alive, connected, and capable of growth. Your emotions are not something to be feared or avoided; they are a vital part of your journey. When you embrace your emotions, you allow yourself to experience life fully, with all its complexities and nuances.

Why All Emotions Matter:

- Joy reminds you of the beauty in the world and fills your heart with light.
- Sadness teaches you about empathy, healing, and the value of what you've lost.
- Anger shows you where your boundaries are and empowers you to stand up for yourself.
- Fear keeps you safe and pushes you to be brave.
- Love connects you to others and makes life richer and more meaningful.
- Confusion nudges you to explore, question, and seek understanding.

Each emotion serves a purpose, helping you navigate the twists and turns of life. By acknowledging and accepting your feelings, you're not just getting through life—you're truly living it.

Accepting and Working with Your Emotions

Accepting your emotions doesn't mean you have to like all of them. It's okay to feel uncomfortable, frustrated, or even scared by certain emotions. What's important is that you don't try to push them away or pretend they don't exist. Instead, try to see your emotions as guides—signals that can teach you something about yourself and the world around you.

Ways to Embrace Your Emotions:

- Name What You're Feeling:
  Sometimes, just putting a name to your emotion can make it feel more manageable. Whether you're feeling excited, nervous, or lonely, acknowledging your feelings is the first step toward understanding them.

- Express Your Emotions:
  Find healthy ways to express what you're feeling, whether it's through talking to someone you trust, writing in a journal, or creating art. Expression is a powerful way to release emotions and gain clarity.

- Allow Yourself to Feel:
  It's okay to feel your emotions fully, even the difficult ones. If you're sad, let yourself cry. If you're angry, find a safe way to release that anger. Giving yourself permission to feel is a crucial part of emotional health.

- Be Compassionate with Yourself:
  Treat yourself with kindness, especially when you're going through tough emotions. Remember that it's okay to struggle and that you're not alone in your feelings. Everyone has their own emotional journey.

- Learn from Your Emotions:
  Every emotion carries a message. What is your anger trying to tell you? What can your sadness teach you about what you value? By reflecting on your emotions, you can gain insights that help you grow.

The Journey Ahead

As you move forward, remember that life is a journey filled with all kinds of experiences—some joyful, some challenging, and everything in between. Your emotions are your companions on this journey, guiding you, teaching you, and helping you navigate the path ahead.

There will be times when your emotions feel overwhelming, and that's okay. It's part of being human. But now, you have tools to help you understand and manage those emotions. You know that it's okay to feel what you're feeling, and that every emotion has value. You're equipped to handle life's ups and downs with resilience and grace.

Embrace the Adventure

Life is full of surprises, and you never know what's around the corner. But that's part of the adventure. Embrace it with an open heart, ready to experience all the emotions that come your way. Each one is a new opportunity to learn more about yourself and to grow into the person you're meant to be.

Believe me when I say…You Are Enough

As you step into the next chapter of your life, take this with you: You are enough, just as you are. Your emotions don't define you, but they do help shape the person you're becoming. Embrace them, learn from them, and use them to guide you on your journey.

Remember, it's okay to feel confused, upset, overwhelmed, happy, excited, and everything in between. These emotions are all part of what it means to be alive, and they're all part of what makes you beautifully, uniquely you.

So go out into the world with courage and curiosity. Embrace every feeling that comes your way, knowing that it's all part of life's rich, colorful tapestry. And never forget—you have the strength and the wisdom to navigate whatever emotions life brings.

A Journey of Growth

As the end of the school year approached, the nine friends—Maya, Emma, Zoe, Lily, Sofia, Kayla, Naomi, Victoria, and Mia—decided to host a small gathering to celebrate their personal growth and the lessons they had learned. Each of them had faced unique emotional challenges over the past year, and this was their chance to come together and reflect on their journey.

The evening was filled with a mix of excitement and nostalgia as they gathered in the school's community center. It was decorated with handmade banners and photos of their various school events and personal milestones. The room buzzed with conversations as they caught up with one another.

Maya, who had learned to understand that everyone faces emotional struggles, was the first to share. "I realized this year that even though it felt like I was the only one struggling with anxiety before big events, all of us have our own challenges. I've learned to be more empathetic and supportive of others."

Emma nodded, adding, "I used to think that maintaining good grades was everything. But I learned that it's okay to feel overwhelmed and that talking to someone can really help. I've started journaling and using grounding techniques, and it's made a huge difference."

Zoe, who had gone through a tough time after a fallout with her best friend, shared her insight. "My grandmother taught me that sadness can lead to personal growth. I've learned that it's okay to grieve and that friendships evolve. Talking about it and finding comfort in small things has helped me heal."

Lily, who had faced self-doubt after criticism on her art, spoke up next. "I've learned that everyone feels self-doubt, even those who seem confident. Embracing my unique style and focusing on my strengths has helped me regain my confidence."

Sofia, who had struggled with feeling left out, added, "I've realized that friendships change over time and it's normal to branch out. Communication is key to resolving conflicts, and it's okay to meet new people and grow."

Emotional Roller Coaster

Kayla, reflecting on her anger and frustration, said, "I learned that channeling my emotions into physical activities and expressing them through words rather than actions is important. It's helped me handle my feelings better and maintain my relationships."

Naomi, who had been on an emotional rollercoaster due to a crush, shared her experience. "I discovered that crushes don't define my worth. Focusing on self-love and maintaining my own identity has made me feel more confident and secure."

Victoria, reflecting on her year of highs and lows, added, "Journaling has been a great tool for me. Looking back at my experiences has shown me how much I've grown. It's helped me approach future challenges with more confidence."

Mia, who had found joy in helping her neighbor despite a tough week, concluded, "I learned that happiness can come from simple, everyday moments. Gratitude and focusing on small joys have really boosted my mood."

As the evening continued, they shared their favorite memories and supported each other in their personal growth. They laughed, reminisced, and celebrated their achievements and progress.

As the night came to a close, the friends gathered for a group photo, capturing the bond they had strengthened through their shared experiences. Each one had faced their own emotional challenges and learned valuable lessons. They understood that emotions are a part of what makes them unique, and that it's important to keep learning, growing, and asking for help when needed.

With a sense of accomplishment and unity, they parted ways, each feeling more confident in their ability to handle future challenges, knowing they had the support of their friends and the wisdom gained from their experiences.

Message: Emotions are a natural part of who we are and learning to navigate them is crucial for personal growth. It's important to keep learning, growing, and not be afraid to ask for help. Celebrating and supporting each other's journeys can strengthen bonds and build confidence for facing future challenges.

Conclusion

Congratulations on taking the time to explore your emotions and learn more about yourself! *Emotional Roller Coaster* is just the beginning of a lifelong journey of understanding and managing your feelings. By working through the activities and reflecting on your experiences, you've already built a stronger connection with your emotions and gained important tools to navigate life's ups and downs.

Remember, it's okay to feel a wide range of emotions—whether they're positive, negative, or somewhere in between. Each feeling has a purpose, and learning to embrace them helps you grow. Whenever you're faced with tough situations or overwhelming feelings, come back to the strategies and exercises you've learned here. Journaling, breathing exercises, and talking things out are all tools you can use at any time.

Emotions are a part of being human, and they don't always make sense. That's okay. What's important is how you respond to them and the steps you take to care for yourself. Keep reflecting, keep expressing, and don't hesitate to reach out to people you trust when you need support.

You've already shown incredible strength by taking this journey, and you have everything you need to continue navigating your feelings with confidence and self-compassion. Know that you are capable of handling whatever emotions come your way.

Acknowledgements

Writing *Emotional Roller Coaster* has been an incredible journey, and I am deeply grateful to those who have supported and inspired me along the way.

First and foremost, I want to thank my family and friends for their unwavering encouragement and love. Your belief in me kept me motivated through every decision I choose. To my mentors and colleagues in the mental health field, your insights have been invaluable in shaping this book and ensuring that it offers meaningful and practical guidance.

A special thank you goes to the teens who shared their experiences and insights with me. Your honesty and courage provided the inspiration and authenticity that are at the heart of this book. I hope this guide serves you well and supports you in understanding and navigating your emotions.

To everyone who contributed to the development and feedback of this project—thank you for your time, thoughtful input, and encouragement. Each of you has played a crucial role in bringing this book to life.

Lastly, I'd like to acknowledge the countless individuals who work every day to support and empower young people. Your dedication and compassion make a profound difference, and this book is a small testament to your important work.

With heartfelt thanks,

Whitney Williams

Resources & Support

Here, you'll find a collection of helpful tools, books, websites, and support services designed to guide you through your emotional journey.

1. ***National Suicide Prevention Lifeline***
    Available 24/7 for crisis support.
    Call: 988
    Website: 988lifeline.org

2. ***Crisis Text Line***
    Free, confidential support via text message.
    Text: HOME to 741741
    Website: [crisistextline.org](https://www.crisistextline.org)

3. ***Teen Line***
    Support and resources for teens dealing with emotional issues.
    Call: 1-800-852-8336
    Website: teenlineonline.org

4. ***National Alliance on Mental Illness (NAMI)***
   Offers education and support for mental health issues.
   Call: 1-800-950-NAMI (6264)
   Website: [nami.org](https://www.nami.org)

5. ***Mental Health America (MHA)***
   Provides tools and information on mental health conditions and resources.
   Website: [mhanational.org](https://www.mhanational.org)

6. ***The Trevor Project***
   Support for LGBTQ+ youth experiencing crisis.
   Call: 1-866-488-7386
   Text: START to 678678
   Website:
[thetrevorproject.org](https://www.thetrevorproject.org)

7. ***ReachOut***
   Resources and support for mental health and well-being.
   Website: [reachout.com](https://au.reachout.com)

8. ***Youth Mental Health Canada***
   Offers resources and support for youth mental health.
   Website: [ymhc.ngo](https://www.ymhc.ngo)

9. ***Headspace***

Guided meditations and mindfulness exercises to help manage stress and emotions.

Website: [headspace.com](https://www.headspace.com)

10. ***Mindfulness for Teens***

Resources and practices for developing mindfulness and managing stress.

Website:

mindfulnessforteens.com

Emotional Roller Coaster

If you or someone you know is struggling with thoughts of suicide, remember that reaching out for help is a sign of strength, not weakness. You are not alone, and there are people who care and want to support you through the darkest moments.

Emotional Roller Coaster